Himalayan Trek
by a
Ten Year Old

This book captures my first Himalayan trek— an unforgettable journey of challenges, perseverance, and personal growth. It reflects on how I pushed through the hardships without giving up, aiming to inspire others to explore, push beyond their limits, and embrace new adventures. It's a collection of my takeaways and cherished memories, preserved to motivate and resonate with fellow explorers.

- Saanvi Mallila

Hi,

I am Saanvi Mallila

About Me

I'm a Pisces and I possess all the qualities of it. I'm empathetic, artistic, emotional and very compassionate. I love to travel and while travelling, I usually prefer to try the local cuisines. By now you might have understood that I'm a foodie. I play keyboard and I'm learning Kuchipudi dance. I'm full of life and a good observer. I usually prefer to stay quiet and people mistake me for an introvert. But, I love to meet new people, make happening conversations and learn new things!

"Kindness is beautiful."

Favorite Colors

My pet

CHAPTERS

Day 1

CHAPTER I

HOW IT ALL BEGAN

5

Few years ago in 2021 , me and my family went on a camping trip with a group called Trekkenture.

It was like a weekend getaway, where we went on a trek to an ancient temple, did rock climbing and camped in the woods for one night.

The weekend trek was very well organised, with proper food and safety, so when the topic of Himalayan trek came up, we were very excited. I throughly enjoyed the bird watching, playing with goats on the way while trekking and the camp was amazing.

We could hear peacocks roaming around our tents in the early hours and I collected lot of peacock feathers as souvenir from this trip.

This wonderful and exciting trek has ignited the desire to go for an Himalayan trek.

CHAPTER II
PACK YOUR BAGS

After 2 years in 2023, we heard that the planning of Himalayan trek to Fungni Top is ready and when we decided to go I jumped at it.

We took a flight from Hyderabad to Delhi. An overnight bus from Delhi to Manali was arranged by the trekking group and all the members are instructed to reach by 4pm at the bus stop to catch this bus. The ride from the airport to the bus stop was no less than an adventure.

We took a cab from the airport to the bus stop, and our driver couldn't seem to understand where we were supposed to go.

We spent about an hour trying to find the bus stop, and the driver wasn't much help. In the meantime, others were sending us photos of themselves at the bus stop, saying that they had reached.

Finally we found the bus stop, and we were super late. Some people from the bus started calling us, saying that the bus driver was making a fuss, and we had to make it quick. We raced to our terminal, and finally found our bus and got on.

I never ran so fast while bumping into people and dragging my luggage. At this point I understood the true meaning of "Less luggage more comfort."

Chapter III
LIFE IN TRANSITION

Finally! We got into the bus. One person told to just sit wherever we found place, because everyone had just switched up their seats, and I settled down with my father.

The bus was very uncomfortable, and the driver was very rash, so nobody got enough sleep that night. Everyone were scared to death by the way he was driving. After about two hours of the bus ride, the driver stopped at a dhaba for dinner.

We had some noodles and momos. We bought some snacks over there, since the bus ride was a long one, and we would need plenty of them. And considering the amount of trekking we were going to do for the next few days, sleep was essential too.

We reached a small inn at about 6:30 in the morning, where we brushed our teeth and had breakfast. The trek organizers were waiting for us there.

They had asked us to carry a quick kit, which consisted of a jacket, a water bottle, some snacks, and medicines in our backpacks.

As my water bottle had broken during the travel, I used my mom's for the rest of the trek. We got our quick kits ready, just as we were about to get in the car for a drive up the mountain to trekking point, it started to rain.

We carried very thin raincoats, which were the use-and-throw kind which turned out absolutely useless for this weather. We tried making some raincoats out of trash bags, which turned out to be kind of a success.

We got in the car, and had a 30-40 minute drive to the trekking point. The view was very beautiful, the mountains with little waterfalls pouring out of them, due to the melted snow. It was mesmerizing.

By the time we reached the start of the trek point, it had stopped raining, and was now sunny. After getting out, they told all the rules about trekking, like how we should breath through our nose and not our mouth, what to do in slippery areas, and more.

Most people were too excited about getting started and were busy clicking pictures instead of listening to the instructions. We started on our trek and it was about an hour up the mountain to base camp. Almost at the end of the trek, my parents sat down for a rest.

They were going to come later, and told me to go with the group. I followed the path and soon caught up with some of the people who were at the end of the line, and made it to base camp with them. My cousins had already reached, so I stayed with them as I waited for my parents.

My parents soon arrived, and they were feeling better now. They were serving some snacks, but I wasn't very hungry. After some time, they called for volunteers to move the luggage from the pully to near the tents.

My father and my uncle went to help, but I stayed back with my mom. After a while they said that we were going on another trek to a valley. All I wanted to do was relax, but it did sound fun. It was a short one compared to the trek to base camp, and towards the end, I slipped!

I would have gone rolling down the edge if my father hadn't caught me just in time. I almost died!

Just kidding! But, would have definitely broken a bone or two. we reached the valley in safety, though. Once we reached the valley we started playing games.

I was in the orange team, and my father as the captain of the opposing team, team, blue. Orange won, but the blue team claimed that we cheated. It did feel to me that we did, sort of. But of course I wasn't going to say it.

By the end of the second round it started to rain. Orange won again. We quickly packed up, started on the trek back to the base camp. We took a shortcut, thankfully. There was a herd of goats, bleating and approaching us. I was anxious to get back to base camp before it got worse, so I stayed with the rest of the line, but by parents were at the back stopping to pet the goats.

I reached the camp and waited for my parents. They reached soon, and more snacks and tea was being served. We ate while they told a little about the trek, and what we were gong to do for the rest of the trek.

They said there was a change in the itenary, we were supposed to go on the trek we just came back from the next day, and go to the top camp on the third day.

But it turns out that the top camp was totally snowed in, and the crew was trying to set it up. They said we would know by tonight, whether we will be leaving tomorrow or day after.

Not a good news for the first day of the trek itself. Later they allotted our tents. My family was put into tent number-2. We took our luggage to the tent, changed and went down to dinner.

They served soup before the actual dinner. we were glad of that, as it was VERY cold. After dinner, everyone retreated to their tents.

Day 2

Chapter IV

The Hard Climb

We woke up pretty early the next morning, or at least it was early for me. Everyone else was up and some were even waiting for breakfast. We brushed our teeth, and since we had changed into todays clothes the night before itself we didn't have to change.

I noticed a few people were still in the clothes from the day before. After breakfast, we packed up our backpacks and got our mule bags out and started our trek to top camp. It was a long and tiring trek of 6-7 hours (depending on how many breaks we took) to top camp.

The younger kids, including my cousin, who is four, had porters so they could be carried over hard parts or when they got tired. I was at the front of the line for more than half the trek. It was very steep at the start, where we had to climb down the mountain we had at our base camp.

After the steep bit it was just a walk on the edge of the mountain for about an hour. I thought the trek was easy up till then, but it soon got much harder.

A shepherd dog had joined us that morning and accompanied us for about a quarter of the trek. It soon saw its herd and went off to them.

We saw some beautiful things on our way, like snow capped mountains, rhododendron flowers, and a variety of animals and birds.

We started from a little ledge near base camp, which was actually scary to walk over for the first time.

 After the path we came to an area with more trees, and it was steeper. There was a herd of wild mules carrying our bags and we saw them on this path.

Apparently one mule got hurt and the rest of them refused to move, so our bags got delivered late to top camp.

We had to cross a huge, dead tree which had fallen when we spotted the mules. We took a lot of breaks while going down this trail eating a bunch of snacks on the way.

After 2 hours we came to a very rocky landscape. This was probably my favourite part. There were tiny waterfalls flowing here and there, with cool and clear water.

We sat down on a few rocks to admire the glorious view of orange-pink clouds around golden mountains, while drinking refreshing water from the springs.

When we got our fill of the view, we continued on our way along the same landscape for approximately another hour.

It was quite an easy trail compared to the previous one. The last and final trail was super steep, almost vertical. So steep we had to tie a rope to two trees and use that to climb.

After that it was still steep, and they served us Tang before the final climb. People started joking about whether we would rather go 5 hours down or 5 minutes up.

My favorite was in a rocky side of the mountain, where we had a wonderful view of the snowcapped mountains.

There were beautiful little streams flowing in the middle of the path, and it was deliciously cool to drink and wash our face.

There was one such stream on the rocky side of the mountain. In the middle of the trek, a bunch of wild mules were racing down the side, and everybody warned us to stay back, and made us cross the over to the other side of a huge fallen tree branch.

Everyone was so happy after we reached top camp. We were all so tired.

As soon as we reached, it started snowing. It was the first time I had seen snowfall in my life (that I can remember), and I was mesmerized.

We all huddled under a tarp that they had put up, to form something similar to a makeshift ceiling.

Everyone put on their raincoats, and while they started a fire under the tarp.

They got the campfire started, and for a few hours everyone just sat near it, while the crew was trying to revive our tents which were buried in snow. We started to play in the snow, which was now piling up. It was soft, but you couldn't really see the designs on the snowflakes, which I was a little disappointed about.

I had seen snow in Kashmir, but there was no snowfall, and the snow over there was like powder. Too small to see any design on it.

After a while, people started saying that they want to go in the tents, but that wasn't possible as it was snowing very heavily, and the crew was still out dusting the snow off the top of the tents.

They told us that, in case it snowed at night, to do the same from inside our tents, pushing the roof up so that the snow fell off.

For hours, it kept snowing, and we all were just sitting there, near the fire, trying to get some warmth. And trust me, its not easy huddled under one tiny tarp, with 35-40 people pushing to get near the fire.

It started to get dark, and still no sign of the snow stopping. There was no electricity and the only light was the campfire. I was feeling very downhearted, wishing I was back home. I began to cry, just like almost every other kid there.

My mom noticed me crying, she came and sat beside me to console me and make me feel better. Everyone was trying to lighten the mood by playing games, like antakshari and after a while they started serving dinner.

They served soup first, of course, but I barely ate anything as I was not at all hungry.

A lot of the kids were very tired, and were just sitting quietly, not playing anything.

My brother had fallen asleep. I wished I could do the same, but it was much too cold for me. It got so dark that you couldn't even see the people who standing farther away from the fire. I couldn't see the tents, or anything beyond the tarp, and i was worried maybe they had blown away. But they hadn't, thankfully.

At about eleven o'clock, we got our tents. Ours had a short climb up a steep bump on the mountain. It was very slippery because of the snow, which still hadn't stopped.

We had sleeping bags which were laid out on top of styrofoam. We kept on shifting the bags around, to make space, because there were six people in the rather tiny tent, excluding my little brother.

Few tents got smashed because of the snow and now we got to adjust for the night with how many people they can accommodate in each tent.

I had to keep moving to make place for others, and my sleeping bag kept slipping off. It took me a while to fall asleep as it was very uncomfortable in the sleeping bag.

I finally fell asleep after about half an hour. I guess day two was the most intense day of our trek.

Day 3

CHAPTER V
BACK TO BASE

When I woke up the next morning I realized my parents had let me sleep in. My brother was already awake and was getting ready to go outside and play. I could hear little kids shouting from the outside about snow and snowmen. I decided to wake up and go outside too. I put my warm gear and shoes on.

When I stepped out of the tent, i was greeted with a blast of warmth, so different from what we experienced the night before. There was a pile of snow next to our tent, though everywhere around it had melted. A bunch of kids were playing in the snow, making snowmen.

The water was freezing cold and the organizers suggested not to brush or wash our face, instead we just gargled with some warm water. I was still drowsy and just ate without even noticing what i was eating.

After breakfast, some people were just sitting around, enjoying the great weather we had today. I went to play in a pile of snow on the other side of our tent.

I threw snowballs at my uncle while he hit them with a plate. After a while they called a vote on who wanted to stay at top camp and who wanted to go back to base camp.

I voted to stay because I didn't feel like I could possibly go back all the way down again. But most of them voted to go down, and majority won.

They said we would start after lunch, because if we started before lunch, they would have to send half their crew down right now to set up for lunch. The organisers made everyone play a game, but I was feeling very tired and sleepy and just wanted to take rest.

After sometime I was feeling better, so I decided to join the next game. It was sort of a shooting game, where when someone's name was called they had to duck, while the people on either side of them shoot at each other.

The one who said "Dish-kaul" the fastest and loudest, won. My cousin brother was upset that he didn't shoot anyone, and began to cry. We spent some time consoling him, and by then the game was over. They took us on another small trek, so that we would get practice going downhill while its slippery.

My mother, my cousin and my aunt didn't come along. It was a very short trek, about fifteen minutes or so. We went to a little ledge, from where we had a beautiful view of the mountains, much better than what we had seen up till then.

We had the view of many more mountains, and the ones in the distance glowed like gold from the light of the sun.

The one even farther back from there, looked like clouds, and they camouflaged perfectly with them. We sat down on the ledge, just admiring the beauty, and then took some pictures.

When we started on our way back it started snowing, but we didn't really feel the the cold, as we were trekking.

It was a little hard on the way back, because the path was even more slippery. When we got back, everyone was around the fire. We had lunch, then got ready to start our trek. They told us a bunch of stuff we needed to know in case we slipped.

We had to put one foot in front and put pressure on the foot behind. Then just let ourselves slide.

 It was very steep and my father helped me most of the way, we crossed the steep part pretty quickly, and before i knew it I found myself on that rocky edge.

We sat down to look at the beautiful view for a while, and then went on our way. I was getting bored, so me and my father played Atlas as we went along. After sometime we were out of reach of the snow. But it was still steep and slippery, as it probably rained in the places where it was not cold enough to snow.

We had some more trekking down, and suddenly the line came to a stop. It turned out that there was a very steep bit and we would need a rope to go down.

They tied a rope to two trees, and we had to hold on to that and walk down.

I had done this before, but uphill. Also then it wasn't muddy, and it was on a rock hill. It took me a while to get the grip right, And I was also nervous, because our body has to face the top while we walk backwards, so you don't know where you're stepping. I almost fell once.

They sent one of the porters behind me to make sure i didn't fall. I made it down, and watched my brother come down with his porter. We had to do it again, and this time I did it with ease. The path looked familiar then, which meant we were close to base camp.

We had some more trekking down, and we saw one of the waterfalls that we saw while going up to top camp.

The ground soon became rocky, instead muddy, and it was flat.

That gave me a boost of energy, and I could run. I went off running and stopped occasionally to let my parents catch up with me.

On the way, me and my parents chatted with one of the other members who were at the back of the line about books and blogs. Soon I got bored and began running again.

They served us tang again, just before a steep part, so that we get energy. The porters were there to help people up. I got to the base camp, and went to the fireplace to sit down. Sometime later they started to serve dinner.

At dinner they told us that we were going to get our mule bags the next day. I kind of wished we could get them now.

We were planning on staying more than one day at top camp, so most of our stuff was in the mule bags.

They also told us that the man who owned the apple orchard we were camping in said that it was the first time in fifty years it snowed in the month of May. FIFTY YEARS!

We ate, and went back into our tents. We didn't know what we were doing the next day. I thought that we were going to go on another small trek, like we went on day one to the valley. I was looking forward to the next day, and soon fell asleep.

Day 4

CHAPTER VI
CHILLAXING

When I woke up, I wasn't feeling very well. My stomach was hurting a lot, and I just laid there in bed for a while. Then I finally got out and brushed my teeth, but I barely ate anything. They said we were going to go rope walking, and it was a small walk to the point. I really wasn't feeling well, so I didn't go.

My mother stayed back with me. I fell asleep after a while, and woke up after an hour or so. They said they would be back in about an hour, and I was pretty sure it had been more than two hours since they left.

The mule bags had arrived, and I went out to get ours. We had three bags in total, and took a while to find. I was feeling like 1 was gonna throw up, so I quickly came back into the tent. I spotted the dog that had accompanied us to top camp near the compost pit.

We waited for some more time and everyone else arrived. It was lunch time then and I still wasn't better. I went to get my food, but the smell just made the sick feeling worse, and I threw up. They said that it was because of staying in the tent for too long. I just wished they had told us that before I spent half the day inside.

I didn't feel like eating anything, and I just had curd rice. They told us to start packing, because we were leaving to Manali the next day. I just sat in the tent, since I couldn't get to sleep. After a while I was feeling better and I ate some snacks that we brought. We just spent the whole of day four lazing out.

We just sat around the fire, chatting. They asked names of the people who wanted to go paragliding. They would arrange for us to go paragliding too, but that would be extra cost.

Me and my family, except my brother decided to go. Basically we just spent the day relaxing and passing time. Then at dinner we had everyone give their introductions. People shared their hobbies, what they did, and some funny stories about themselves.

It was so fascinating to hear their stories, adventures and getting to know so much about trekking and other things. This was the best part of the day. I gave my introduction after my family and said that I'm a Kuchipudi dancer, played keyboard, and was getting trained in tennis. After my introduction I went to the tent, because they were setting the food up, and the smell made me feel sick.

I came out after a while for dinner, but I still ate curd rice. After a while, we went into our tents and began packing what was left out. Then we went to sleep. Day 4 was the least happening day.

Day 5
PASSPORT
43

CHAPTER VII
BACK IN THE CITY

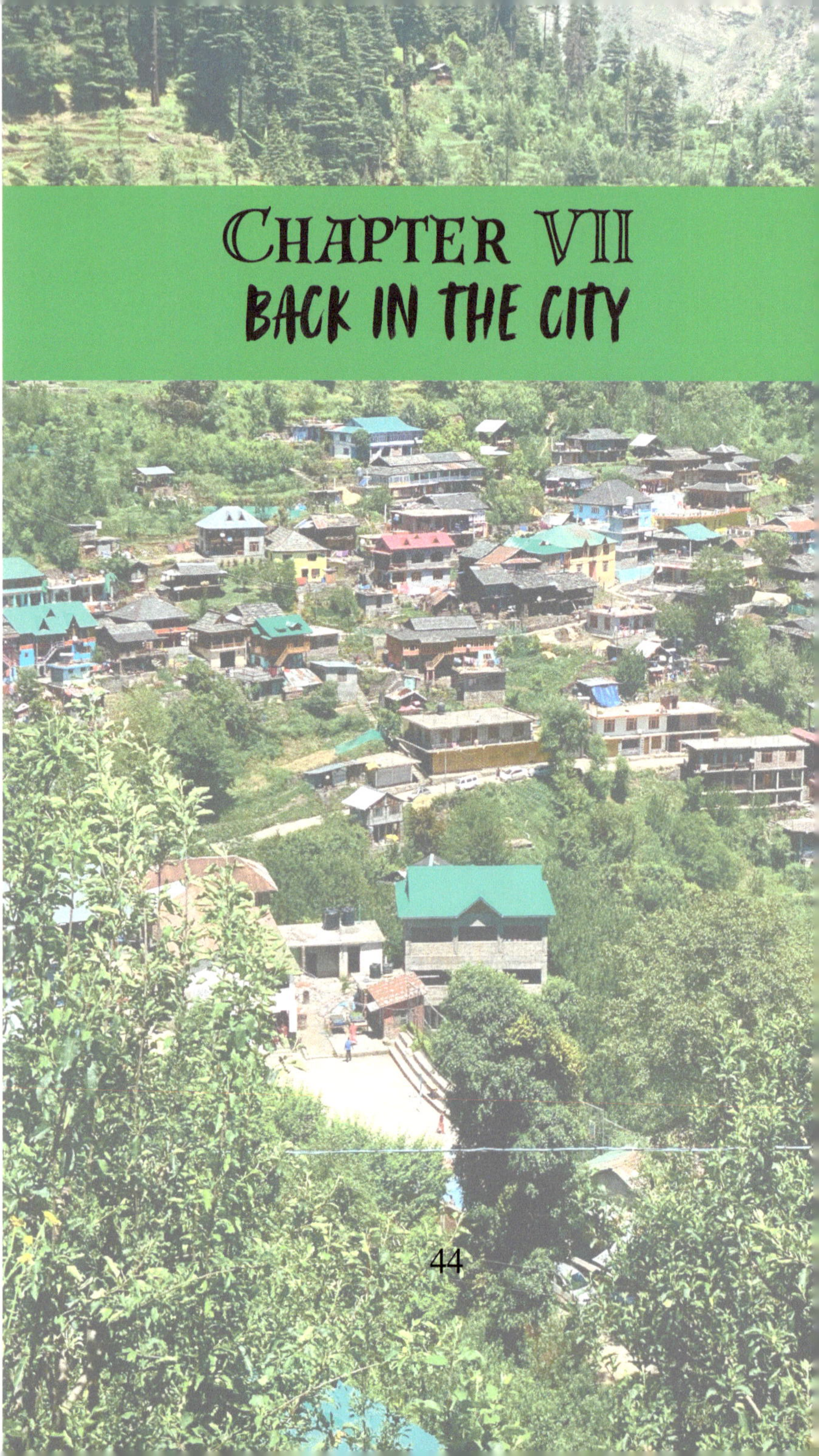

We woke up at around 7:00 or 7:30. We were going to Manali! I was so happy. I was feeing much better now, and I was able to eat a little more than the day before. Everyone was in a good mood and excited. My family, especially, because we were going paragliding. They confirmed whoever was going paragliding, by reading out the list they had wrote day before, and asking if anyone else wanted to come.

One or two other people signed up too, and we went back to our tents to pack our backpacks, as there were still some odds and ends lying around. We gathered near the starting point, and they give us certificates.

It said UNSTOPPABLE YOU on it. I got it signed by the trek leader, and one of the assistants. Then we had the trek down again. They took us the same route for some time, then shifted us to a shortcut.

On the way we met a old woman, who said something I couldn't understand. She is the mother of the orchard owner. I was amazed to see her walk up the hill at ease at that age. We continued down the path and soon came to the road we were dropped off on day 1.

We had to wait for the vehicles to arrive and we spent the time taking selfies and pictures of the amazing scenery.

The trek leader was staying back at Manali along with the organizers, to wait for the next batch, so we took group selfies and pictures with them.

One of the organizers, who was also a photographer, found a lizard perfectly blended into the rocky mountain wall on the side of us. It took me quite some time to see it. The cabs came soon, and then we had to wait for the luggage to come by the pully.

Fortunately they didn't take long, and we were soon busy loading the luggage into the cars. My mother, uncle, aunt, and cousin sat at the back. There wasn't any more space so I sat in the front with my father.

It was a little uncomfortable, but after a while we got used to it. We went down the mountain, and all the while my father talked to the driver about the best places to see.

The driver owned the apple orchard we were camping in, and he was very enthusiastic to hear about our trek. He said that we could go to the Atal Tunnel, which was the longest tunnel in the world (11 km), going through the mountains.

On the other side there would be an amazing view of the mountains surrounding us. We couldn't go paragliding that day, because the wind was blowing in the wrong direction.

Nobody was hungry, as we were munching on all kinds of snacks we could find, so we didn't stop to eat.

It took us about an hour and a half to reach the Atal Tunnel, as we went there first. It was about a ten minute drive through the tunnel.

I didn't like it much. We had to keep our windows up and it was very suffocating as we were going through the mountains.

After we came out, I was very relieved, as now we could have the windows down. We took some pictures, and then went back to the car. There was a man with a mountain rabbit over there. I held it and took a picture. It was super furry and soft.

We piled back into the car, and made our way to Rohtang Pass. We were going there because there was an amazing view on top.

We went to the base of the Rohtang Pass, and our driver went to get permission to go all the way up Rohtang Pass. In the meantime we ate some maggi and drank tea for a sort of lunch/snack.

We chatted with some of the people who were there on our trek. They said that they were waiting since a very long time to go up, but they weren't allowing them.

Our driver came back after a while, and said that we didn't get permission to go all the way, but just a little bit of the way.

We were disappointed, but at least we would see the view. We took the 2-minute drive up the mountain, and came about a quarter of the way up. The view was certainly spectacular, like the amazing snowcapped mountains were right beside us.

We took some pictures, and my father found a small waterfall made from the melted snow.

We were looking for him to take a group picture, and I spotted him over near the waterfall taking pictures of the scenery. I called him for the picture, but he beckoned for me to join him.

The driver was motioning for us to not go there, but I ignored him, as my father was still calling me. I got an awesome picture in front of the mountains.

The driver was telling us to come back so we could start on the way down, so we took the last group picture and went back to our car.

We started on our way down to the village, and as it was getting dark, we decided to go back to our hotel.

After we checked in, we took our first bath in five days, it felt so good. Then we just watched TV for a while, and we ordered dinner to our room.

My aunt and uncle, who were in the room beside ours, came into our room to eat. We were all super tired, and decided to go to bed as soon as possible.

Everyone soon completed, and we went to sleep, after browsing all the TV channels and finding nothing interesting. Day 5 was fun, but I'm just happy we got to take a bath.

Day 6

Chapter VIII
Sightseeing

We woke up a little late the next morning, and my mom was not feeling well. I didn't want to get out of bed, but I finally dragged myself to the bathroom, and brushed my teeth.

I took a bath, and then got ready in our matching T-shirts. My cousins were waiting outside and father said to go along with them to breakfast, and he would join me in a while. We had toast, dosa, and idly. The dosa and idly were not so great as we were in the north, as that is the south cuisine. I had to have some milk, so I had it mixed with some chocolate syrup.

My father came down and said he was going to take the breakfast up to my mom, as she was not feeling well, and told us to go out on our own, and if she was feeling better by afternoon she would join us.

Me and my uncle had spotted a board game area in the lobby, and went to play while my father checked what all we could do. we played football and chess.

Soon it was time to leave, and we were first going to a temple of Hidimbi. when we got there I noticed it was kind of like a fair, and there were yak rides, from the drop-off area to the gate.

I rode on the yak, and it was super bumpy, but I enjoyed it. My cousin was too scared to go and started crying if someone tried to make him ride.

When inside the temple, we saw that there were different stalls with games, lambs and mountain rabbits you could hold, and all kinds of shops. I wanted to play a game, but we had to go and see the actual temple first.

We walked through all the shops and stalls and made our way to the temple, only to find that it had a line stretching halfway around it, we took some pictures near it and went to play in the stalls.

I fed a rabbit, and held a lamb, and tried a ring toss game, archery, and a game where you had to knock down all the cups. I didn't win anything, but it was fun to play anyway. Then we went back to the hotel for lunch, as we didn't want to leave my mom alone for long.

My father called my mom and she said she would get ready and come downstairs, we ordered some curd rice for my mom, and biryani for the rest of us.

My uncle and I went to play the board games while we waited for the food.

My uncle got a call he thought it was the others calling to say the food had arrived, so we went back to the dining room. But it turned out to be only an office call.

We didn't go back again, as we had already reached the dining room. About two minutes after we came, our food arrived. We started on our biryani, and waited for my mom to come. She soon came, and we quickly completed our meal.

We decided not to go paragliding at all, because the winds weren't good again. We decided to go on the hot air balloon instead.

We went on the drive to the Beas river, as the driver said that there was a hot air balloon on the shore of the river. I got nervous by looking at it, as it didn't seem safe. But my parents said it was fine and perfectly safe.

I got even more nervous as we boarded it. I stood next to my father, and I noticed that the gas from the fire on top was leaking.

The heat and tremendous sound from the fire didn't help either. We went up in the air but they pulled it down because something was wrong with the air direction.

I was very glad of that. After we got down we had run out of the way, otherwise the balloon would have fallen on us.

My parents were pretty enthusiastic about it, but I was now terrified of it, and I wouldn't go on, nor did I want my parents to.

But they went on and came down perfectly safe, but I still didn't want to go on. We took some pictures near the river, and then went to have dinner.

We wanted to try the local food, so we went to a dhaba to try fish fry. There were some games there too, and we played in little boats you could row and archery.

There were more games too, like the huge bubble that you go in, and there was a bridge, but we hadn't eaten yet and we might get sick if we went in the bubble.

It was too dark, anyway. Then we went and waited for our food. It soon came and we ate it contentedly.

We thought we would go to mall road to do some shopping if it wasn't too late, but it was already very dark, so we decided to go back to the hotel, have some light dinner, and go to sleep. We made our way back to the hotel, and ordered some curd rice. We ate quickly and went to sleep.

Day 7

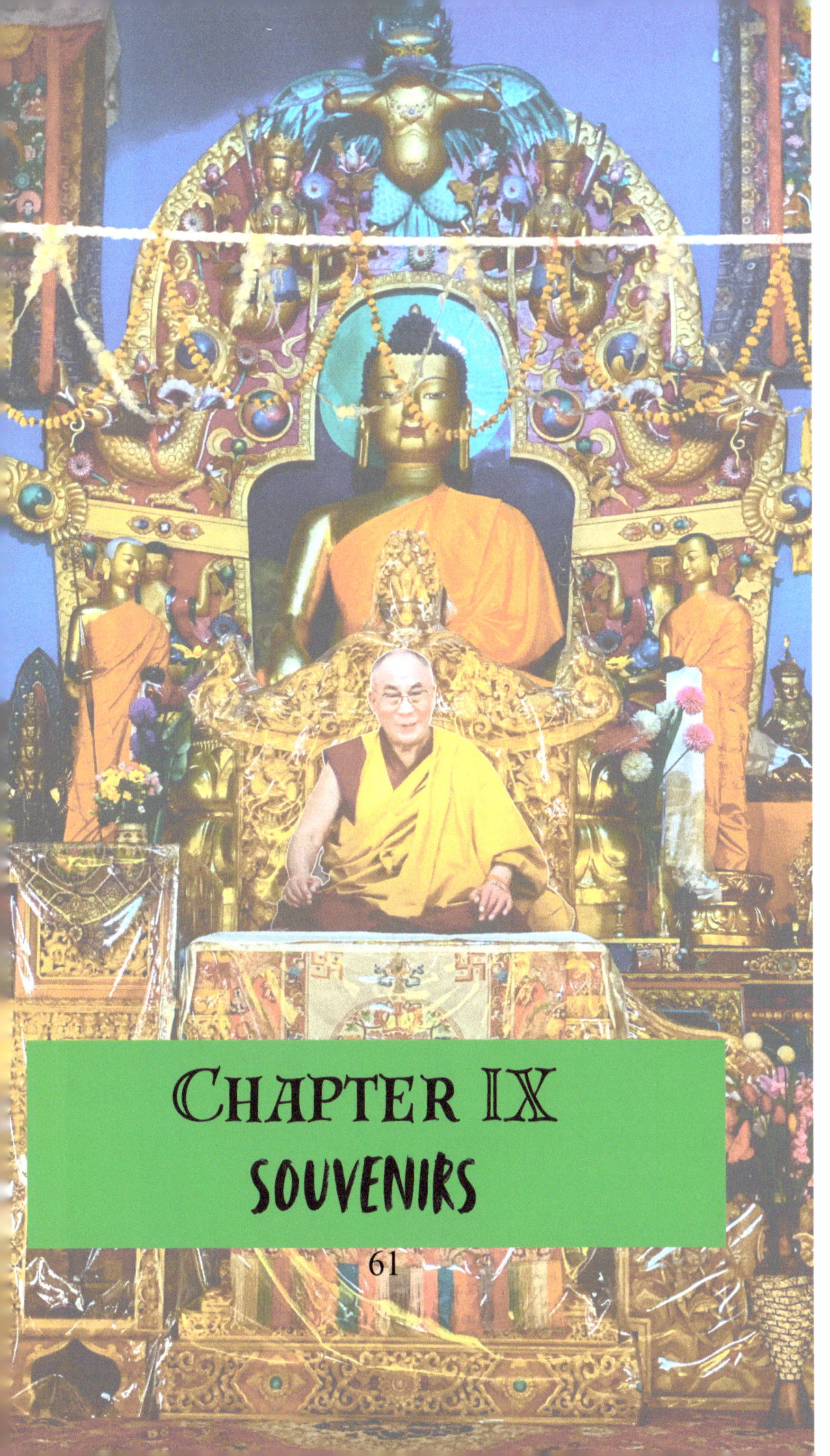

CHAPTER IX
SOUVENIRS
61

When we woke up the next day I was excited because we were going to go to mall road. I got into my favorite top. We went downstairs for breakfast, and it wasn't much different from what what we ate the day before, except it was french toast instead of toast.

We were first going to a monastery, and it was a few hours drive from our hotel. We started kind of late, at about 11:30. I almost fell asleep on the way. Once we reached, we had to take off our shoes before going in, and there was a big curtain hanging in front of the door.

"YOU MAY GO UNDER CURTAIN" said a sign next to it. I followed my father under it. Once inside, there was a huge cardboard cutout of Dalai Lama, who the monastery was dedicated to, and for a second I thought it was a real person.

My father told me his story as we took pictures inside. It was a little hostel, for people who wanted to become monks. There was a little shop over there and we bought some snacks, and my mom bought some incense sticks.

We started on our way to mall road, where we planned to spend the rest of the day, shopping and eating.

On the way our driver asked us if we wanted to see a tiny waterfall, and we decided to go. It was on the way, on the side of the road, and we took pictures on a bridge going across.

It was a very tiny waterfall, and almost couldn't be called one, it was more like a tiny stream. My feet had gotten completely wet, and I didn't want to wear my socks on top of them, so we decided to wait for a while.

We bought some cool drinks at a shop nearby, and started on our way to Mall road.

It was about 3:00 now, and we decided to have lunch first. It took us an hour to reach mall road and when we did, we went to a cafe, which a lot of our friends from the trek had recommended.

The food was certainly good, and there was live music. We ate leisurely and after we completed, we decided to start our shopping.

As soon as we went out of the cafe, we ran into some of our friends from the trek. We talked for a while, and then started our shopping.

There were all kinds of shops there, from jewelry, to keychains, to softies. I have a keychain collection, and wherever we go, I collect a keychain.

And this time was no different. I got a custom-painted keychain, with my name on one side and "Manali 2023" with a tree on the other side. I was happy to get that done right away.

I was thinking of starting a earring collection too, and I also wanted a matching set of evil eye jewelry. I found earrings for a serious discount (they were 150 rupees, but I got them for 50 rupees), then I went looking for a bracelet.

I wanted to get them from a different shop, since I didn't think the woman I got the earrings from would give me any other discount.

There was a shop that sold softies next to us, so I got a vanilla one, we continued roaming around and my parents looked for a magnet that showed trekking in Manali.

They soon found one and we went to check out a room decor shop. There was some amazing room decor there, but it was too expensive and out of my budget. We decided to move on, and I went back to the shop where I got the earings to see if they had bracelets.

They did, but each one was 100 rupees, and that was all I had left in my budget. 1 decided to take it, as I couldn't find any necklaces.

Anyway, we got some popcorn and waited for my cousins in front of the cafe we had eaten in. They soon arrived and we waited for our car.

I was contended with what I bought, and I couldn't wait to try on the earrings. We reached our hotel, and we weren't hungry, since we had such a late lunch.

We just ate some curd rice, and went to bed early. We had to wake up at 5:00 the next day, because we had our flight at 12:00, and it was a 6-7 hour drive to the airport from our hotel.

I fell asleep pretty quickly, as I was tired out with all our walking around in mall road. I enjoyed day 7.

Day 8
PASSPORT

CHAPTER X
HOME SWEET HOME

I woke after my parents, and I found that everything was already packed. All 1 had to do was brush my teeth. My father and uncle had gone downstairs to check out of the hotel. I got ready, grabbed my backpack, and we went downstairs.

Our driver was waiting outside for us, and we got into the car. This time I sat all the way at the back, with my mom. I slept in her lap, and after a while we stopped at a little snack place at about 7:00. The grown ups got some tea, and we bought some chips and biscuits. I just wanted to get back to my nap. When we reached the airport, we quickly checked in our luggage and sat down to wait.

Some people from our trek, the same people we had run into yesterday, arrived at the airport too. I sat chatting with one of them, who was a few years older than me.

After a while we had to go, as it was time for our flight. We first went to have lunch, and then boarded our flight. I fell asleep on the flight, and it was dark by the time we reached Hyderabad.

I enjoyed the trip a lot, but in the end, there's no place like **HOME**.

Conclusion

CHAPTER XI
TAKEAWAYS
73
7 May 2

Through out the trek, I certainly felt like I can't, won't, and that I just wanted to go home. But through this trek I have learnt how to push myself, and never give up.

I'm glad that I went on this trek, because if I didn't, I never would have learnt the things no book can ever teach me.

I would have never realized how strong I was and how strong my will power is. I learned the ways of nature and how unpredictable the weather was. I developed a deep connection with the nature and now when I recall my Himalayan trek, I feel amazed with all the things I have done.

The days with extreme weather conditions, no cozy beds to sleep in, tired body, no hot showers made me realize how we ignore and take it for granted of all the comforts we are provided back home.

I'm so grateful that I got a chance to experience all this only to appreciate everything I have and received.

THE END